INNOCENCE

INNOCENCE

FIRST EDITION

Copyright © 2022 Michael Joseph Walsh

Printed in the United States of America
ISBN 978·1·7348167·5·4

DESIGN ≈ SEVY PEREZ
Brandon Grotesque & Adobe Caslon Pro

This book is published by the

Cleveland State University Poetry Center
csupoetrycenter.com
2121 Euclid Avenue, Cleveland, Ohio 44115-2214

and is distributed by

SPD / Small Press Distribution, Inc.
spdbooks.org
1341 Seventh Street Berkeley, California 94710-1409

A CATALOG RECORD FOR THIS TITLE IS
AVAILABLE FROM THE LIBRARY OF CONGRESS

INNOCENCE

MICHAEL
JOSEPH WALSH

國破山河在

The country is broken; the mountains and rivers remain.

—Du Fu

INNOCENCE

So the drawing moves
in the space that resembles air.
So the adventure of intricacy smiles
one time finally, then is gone.

There is another logic
by night, no flowers.
There is other than me
stretched out in the fabric of voice

to clothe and adorn
this secret. And whatever spills
into the present is the thing that will last.
And the world whose clichés we awakened is already
    far behind us.

But only faintly, held up unto music:
to let usage guide desire,
to let the dream cut
from the body form all four walls.

We too have our associations,
our immanence along the horizon
as it muscles from red to green.
And so sweetly then,

to give in to that failure:
on the one hand what one is,
on the other its opposite future,
which surrounds us now, and is our world.

The stars fall, a love of ugliness
warms the throat. And whoever would not
be embedded in that house is left to call out "Who?",
open mouth to the wind.

From the end of that human
possession to be not sweet enough,
to grow bad in the good light,
in the exhaust cloud of art.

There are many ways,
there is more than one way.
To say the book is all lies,
to say the market is no longer

a money bag, to say a factory symbol
will be the measure of the growth of, say,
the factory image as it swells across
all dimensions.

Now picture a money bag
of similar proportions,
your son or daughter
semi-attached as products of that state.

There are more of us than there used to be.
To make the right
decisions we need to look at things
in different locations, returning home to mourn

the loss of being emplaced and alive,
rearing up thus large in spirit
to solve the problem of a life
whose size no longer serves us.

A volcano of oil is flowing,
and we believe in it,
and call it our innocence.
We admire ourselves

amongst ourselves, not denying
the derisory squeals
into which our avatars
plunge. For this is the minute in all its voice

which would be sweet, and swallow our hearts.
Coherence is thick, time
is thick, reality
is cruel and knows us

for our danger,
which is fashionable now,
and will predict our slow end.
Someday something

(as I write this I want)
someday something
will happen. And when it is cold,
when it is warm,

there is a taste we will share
for a science that speaks
a cloud for every possible face, a body
for nature gutting itself to shine

only now and then at first, then always
(to quote the voice) as the golden
poem "I am breathing," the moaning of
the I who meets the eye

in the evaporating pool.
Because it is cruel to live,
and crueler, on this earth which is
an entire body of cherished

affinity wet feet and air, not to,
because the condition of permanent
crisis we hold
inside ourselves remembers us

in the egg of our eventual deaths,
I will write this as it occurs
though cold and teeming, though florid
with pictures destroying the cared-for air,

until my hands go still
(thus crueler), and April is torn
back into words we know—
and by this what affections new

shall summon us,
what screams become
economies within
and seed the air with impossible sound.

I.

놀이터 (PLAYGROUND)

"시장은 철없는 아이들의 놀이터가 아니다"라고 그는 취임사에서 말했다.

어떤 장애물이든 극복할 만큼 그걸 간절히 원하는가?

장래에 대한 달콤한 환상은 사라지고 피의 보복을 다짐한다. 그 노래를 들으면 들을수록 새로운 느낌이 든다.

어떤 장애물이든 극복할 만큼 그걸 간절히 원하는가? 그 날개들은 포옹의 감각을 나타내기 위해 앞으로 살짝 치우쳐져 있다.

장래에 대한 달콤한 환상은 사라지고 피의 보복을 다짐한다. 기슭에 출렁거리는 물결, 바람이 꽉 찬 돛폭 같은 너의 어깨.

그 날개들은 포옹의 감각을 나타내기 위해 앞으로 살짝 치우쳐져 있다. 재앙은 돌고 돌아 축복이 된다: 뱀 모양의 형상, 지그재그선, 새 한 마리.

기슭에 출렁거리는 물결, 바람이 꽉 찬 돛폭 같은 너의 어깨. 조리 된 사과에 설탕과 계피를 첨가한다. 외양과 실제가 들어맞는 경우는 좀처럼 없다.

재앙은 돌고 돌아 축복이 된다: 뱀 모양의 형상, 지그재그 선, 새 한 마리.

그렇기 때문에 어느 하나가 다른 하나에 의존한다고 말할 땐 항상 주의해야 한다.

조리 된 사과에 설탕과 계피를 첨가한다. 외양과 실제가 들어맞는 경우는 좀처럼 없다.

그 다음날 아침, 우리는 그것이 해골에 고인 썩은 물이라는 것을 발견했다.

그렇기 때문에 어느 하나가 다른 하나에 의존한다고 말할 땐 항상 주의해야 한다.

"시장은 철없는 아이들의 놀이터가 아니다"라고 그는 취임사에서 말했다.

그 다음날 아침, 우리는 그것이 해골에 고인 썩은 물이라는 것을 발견했다.

그 노래를 들으면 들을수록 새로운 느낌이 든다.

PLAYGROUND (놀이터)

after John Yau

"The market is not a playground for thoughtless children,"
    he said in his inaugural speech.
Do you want it desperately enough to overcome any obstacle?

My sweet visions of the future vanish, I pledge myself to bloody
    revenge.
The more I hear that song the newer it feels to me.

Do you want it desperately enough to overcome any obstacle?
The wings are angled forward slightly to create a sense of embrace.

My sweet visions of the future vanish, I pledge myself to bloody
    revenge.
Little waves lapping against the shore, your shoulders like a sail
    full of wind.

The wings are angled forward slightly to create a sense of embrace.
Disaster rolls over and becomes a blessing: a snake-shaped figure,
    a zigzag, a bird.

Little waves lapping against the shore, your shoulders like a sail
    full of wind.
I add the sugar and cinnamon to the cooked apples.
    Appearance and reality seldom correspond.

Disaster rolls over and becomes a blessing: a snake-shaped figure,
    a zigzag, a bird.
So be careful when you say that one thing depends upon another.

I add the sugar and cinnamon to the cooked apples.
    Appearance and reality seldom correspond.
The next morning we learned it was only rotten water in a skull.

So be careful when you say that one thing depends upon another.
"The market is not a playground for thoughtless children,"
    he said in his inaugural speech.

The next morning we learned it was only rotten water in a skull.
The more I hear that song the newer it feels to me.

OWNERSHIP

Conspiracy is a science
that speaks cloud,

as I remember it.
& viral is that cloud's

fine hand over the loved
personae of our dead.

Everyone you know is
every word aloud

in your head
(& rare to see)

(to form the words),
to purr deeply,

all the names
set in motion by

what it is to us
in intimate stone.

It's not easy
(it gives him images),

shadow of a dog
by the riverbank,

the heavy head
of the future in which

these incapacities
swell. When they are mature,

when the flow is a wolf like this
& true enough,

on the round earth
with the side of its eye,

to have been this
beautiful, pathless

& thus marked
out of today

& into some golden
coherence

which is the violent perception
of a mistake.

So the change comes
always against the wind,

& the facts that crowd
the ugly present take heart

("A snout" "No, nothing")
& uphold such blessings as these

which in time become our secrecy.
To say this shadow is mine

& also mine,
& so it happened here,

where we rose
together to the surface of the mind
as wind through a rent
umbrella does

my thinking for me, & rises sweet
from the ruins of a life

in which we know to let
our manor sound

inside us,
our stronger voice

become a dream of ownership,
where the waves are born

of collective flesh,
where more is made

of love than of
our empty mourning,

money that pillows
the void & is our ghost.

FORTY DAYS

At one point I dreamt
I was getting the better of this.
I had been breathed on at least
in another age. Time flows

into the sleepless joint of the poem,
the small life of these words,
the melted year.
& light will open

& the eye will
pursue bravely this ugly motif,
going there, without us,
in sickness, remembering health

in its varieties half-
viscous a dozen names
left on a surface
for twelve hours, thirty, a year.

That I have swallowed something
worth the while, let that be the record of my love.
Let a language build up
as this image wears away.

Next June I will touch your face,
strange friend.
This is a story I've already dreamed.

COMMON FLOWERS

You can grow some things,
whether you want them or not.
The air that surrounds us here we call music,

the force of which is old, and full of life.
It imagines us here, and finds pleasure in the shape of our wound.
The door is open, and above and about

the common flowers the adventure of prolonging
other logics spreads weakly in two directions.
To this I give myself, and it heals me,

reinfects me with the shape of this place.
I sleep, I form opinions. When it rises to the surface of the mind,
        I greet the sun.

How otherwise should I have devised this dance of omission?
To falter before the building,
to fall over every inch of it.

And thus the music lives,
the ghosts wind up the spirit;
shortcuts to pleasure, wounded springs.

But what happens tomorrow will change all that,
like a diamond left out in the cold.
And yet I would, if you wished,

tear a hole in this fabric we've made,
and so distend the earth,
and grow drunk on our non-continuance. The cipher burns

slowly the thing it pleases,
and this is knowing, but like the heart not knowing quite how.
The waves breathe long, and the smell of earth

in the half-shade points to a sex that would be myriad,
and shimmer, and derive from touch
what in stillness will come to pass—

here where the wind blows, and a body lives,
and where the grasses that are not dead
will tell the story of what that means.

FORECAST

If each of us is arriving
now under the sign of feeling,

which here in sweet
eerie thoughtlessness is
constellated as the knowledge of evil,

then we can say that what arises
in the shadow of that
cross-eyed star is what

saying nothing means
in the context of this recording:
this territory
that would be our friend

& in the fruit
of our split would call out from that whorl
which in summer I remember & in winter I
put deep back in the ground.

This is what it means to live
without figure, between oneself, having passed
from speech to warm
presence without first

(& this is the miracle)
having with dim dis-
connectedness poured the juice of that meat
out into the paid-for air.

The light that spills
through the window is warm,
& crushes this image,
& with a careful human

glance embeds its name in the dark,
then swallows us whole.
What follows from this
expands as a feeling arises:

that you will meet me on that ground, or find me
before one order
of feeling folds into its brethren,
fact of that ugly future, sunlight
over the bed with stillness & broken glass.

& so what I seek
I experience constantly.
& love is here, & toward me

the danger that wakes the day's swallowed back, candle
that turns its light from mirror
to bitten mouth.
It is already a world,

this hybrid machine.
It is the prettiest
ambrosial flower, fluid-soaked
& normal.

& one connects with this
the raw night
one has a fondness for,

the animal that in its walking conceals
what gentleness, luxuriant cruelty,
which is the story of every accessible form.
The day is long,

it fills up with paper.
The program to which I submit myself
grows murky.
It forecasts this very dream.

본국 (NATIVE COUNTRY)

본국에 돌아가거들랑 편지해요.
모든 비극은 여기서부터 시작되고, 그것은 아름다운 음악으로 승화된다.

그렇지만 사물의 거죽만 보거나 자정에 계단을 내려가면서 거울을 들여다본다.
직접 피로한 몸으로. 기쁠 때나 슬플 때나 피부를 위한 페인트이다.

모든 비극은 여기서부터 시작되고, 그것은 아름다운 음악으로 승화된다.
묘소를 찾는것은 언어가 사상의 기호인 것처럼 만물이 다시 소생할 것이라는 약속이다.

직접 피로한 몸으로. 기쁠 때나 슬플 때나 피부를 위한 페인트이다.
혼자 있을 때에는 누구이거나 간에 문을 열어 주지 않는다.

묘소를 찾는것은 언어가 사상의 기호인 것처럼 만물이 다시 소생할 것이라는 약속이다.
그리고 전세계의 이목이 쇠사슬에 묶인 죄수인 당신에 집중되어 있다.

혼자 있을 때에는 누구이거나 간에 문을 열어 주지 않는다.
두 강은 이 지점에서 합류한다. 군중은 회관 안으로 한꺼번에 밀려온다.

그리고 전세계의 이목이 쇠사슬에 묶인 죄수인 당신에 집중되어 있다.

밟아서 다져진 길, 백지 한 장, 눈을 더럽게 하는 그을음과 재.

두 강은 이 지점에서 합류한다. 군중은 회관 안으로 한꺼번에 밀려온다.

각기 다른 외형과 생김새를 분석하여 하나를 다른 하나로부터 구분한다.

밟아서 다져진 길, 백지 한 장, 눈을 더럽게 하는 그을음과 재.

본국에 돌아가거들랑 편지해요.

각기 다른 외형과 생김새를 분석하여 하나를 다른 하나로부터 구분한다.

그렇지만 사물의 거죽만 보거나 자정에 계단을 내려가면서 거울을 들여다본다.

NATIVE COUNTRY (본국)

When you get back to your native country, write me a letter.
All tragedy starts from here, then is sublimated into beautiful music.

But you look only into the surfaces of things, or into mirrors,
    walking downstairs at midnight.
In person, to the tired body. This is a paint for the skin, in good
    times and in bad.

All tragedy starts from here, then is sublimated into beautiful music.
To visit the graves is a promise that everything will come alive once
    again, as words are the signs of ideas.

In person, to the tired body. This is a paint for the skin, in good
    times and in bad.
When you're alone, you don't open the door for anyone (no matter
    who it might be).

To visit the graves is a promise that everything will come alive once
    again, as words are the signs of ideas.
Then the eyes of the world are centered on you, a criminal in chains.

When you're alone, you don't open the door for anyone
  (no matter who it might be).
The two rivers meet at this point, the crowd surges into the hall.

Then the eyes of the world are centered on you, a criminal in chains.
The beaten path, the sheet of blank paper, the soot and ash dirtying
  the snow.

The two rivers meet at this point, the crowd surges into the hall.
We distinguish one from another by analyzing their different
  motions and shapes.

The beaten path, the sheet of blank paper, the soot and ash dirtying
  the snow.
When you get back to your native country, write me a letter.

We distinguish one from another by analyzing their different
  motions and shapes.
But you look only into the surfaces of things, or into mirrors,
  walking downstairs at midnight.

THERE IS A BODY INSIDE EXPERIENCE

Whichever piece of the heart this is,
it peoples this little book.

Its circle is vaguely fated like a touch from whatever destroys.
& in this way it draws you up,

from these depths which are depths,
& blue lips, like waving grasses.

& in this way the mud that shapes the brain
in hybrid thicket is the warmth one feels,

without hands, & holding pressure,
& every technique has reason & even the birds would die
    to know.

DRONE OF ART

But not everyone speaks
the language we speak.

It is insane to know both
(as everyone touches)

the smooth brown fur,
the cobwebs spreading

across the faces of two clay cherubim,
"some drone of art"
that awakens a world.

We'll see it out. We'll call it our own
subterranean, the warm suede
glove of the monitored life.

The lived is the new
virtual, the virtual the new set
object of our satisfaction, what we call
in winter quarters the blood

("Say now unchanged")
is set round with flowers
that glow with a different light.

What you see is but half
the operation of this device.
I, whose life was but yesterday, I who

instead of flowers underfoot,
with the miserable truth, I who live
in bits and pieces, would very
slowly on this vast

stage dissociate from both
the meat and the blood,
the sun that pours
digitally over the rhyme of one's blinking corpse.

The machine resembles
our opinions of ourselves.
The atmosphere is full,
monosyllables

pierce the eye, the clouds glow
with pointless courage and in hours will
explode. Can we be happy?
That this I is also,

in this instant, speaking,
can we countenance that?
Of selves unable to recall
themselves, to tell that story,

of the perfect bestial
flower in which a person grows
too old to die. Or how in that sweet

break in the personal
such a creature took shape
and somehow oozed on.

MERIDIAN

This feeling at least is certain.
I walk slowly alongside it.
One part is sickness,
one is intimacy

that walks in the sun,
a thin and vast
undulation
to which people speak,

or the closed eyes
of the lake that turn
me out of myself
and set no limit to love.

Just as *the scenery,*
when it is truly seen,
reacts on the life of the seer,
so the beloved's

gait becomes clear to you
and shatters the smooth body of the crowd.
What I'm saying is,
our hells are not the same.

In autumn
when one has the strength,
in spring when one crawls
out of the sun

and into the lake, the truth
is one jerky step, is a mode
of sleep less light more flesh,
where the usual things

have density,
and over the churning
oil you feel the eyes of all you wanted
fixed on you.

In the end what stands out is the green mountain,
the cloud drifting across it.
Let everyone live, let no one
disappear.

Let the blood walk
its slow loop around its meridian,
and the flowers keep time for us,
opening and closing their mouths.

The measured earth is neither whole,
nor shadow of a whole.
All mountains are polyglots.

And though the sun is hot,
and though I tremble,
let those gates slide open for me.

극락 (PURE LAND)

보시다시피, 우리는 어려운 처지에 놓여 있었다.
노인은 두 손을 모아 사후의 극락왕생을 빌었다.

죽자니 청춘이고, 살자니 고생이다. 그렇다고 생각했다.
너무 반가우면 눈물이 났다.

노인은 두 손을 모아 사후의 극락왕생을 빌었다.
새끼로 개의 목을 옭더니 그윽한 장미꽃 향기에 나 자신을 잊었다.

죽자니 청춘이고, 살자니 고생이다. 그렇다고 생각했다.
알고 있는데도 모르는 체 하더라고요.

새끼로 개의 목을 옭더니 그윽한 장미꽃 향기에 나 자신을 잊었다.
노래하랴, 춤추랴 숨이 꽤 찼겠네!

알고 있는데도 모르는 체 하더라고요.
내 차례구나 싶자 막 떨리더군요.

노래하랴, 춤추랴 숨이 꽤 찼겠네!
새가 울고, 꽃이 피었다. 하늘은 높고, 바다는 깊었다.

내 차례구나 싶자 막 떨리더군요.
너무 웃어서 배가 다 아팠다.

새가 울고, 꽃이 피었다. 하늘은 높고, 바다는 깊었다.
보시다시피, 우리는 어려운 처지에 놓여 있었다.

너무 웃어서 배가 다 아팠다.
너무 반가우면 눈물이 났다.

PURE LAND (극락)

As you can see, we were now facing a difficult situation.
The old man pressed his hands together and prayed for rebirth
    in the Pure Land.

I thought, perhaps I'll die, but I'm still so young; I thought,
    perhaps I'll live, but life is suffering.
When I was very pleased to see someone, I cried.

The old man pressed his hands together and prayed for rebirth
    in the Pure Land.
In the fragrant roses I forgot myself, having tied a rope round
    the neck of the dog.

I thought, perhaps I'll die, but I'm still so young; I thought,
    perhaps I'll live, but life is suffering.
I pretended not to know, despite the fact that I knew.

In the fragrant roses I forgot myself, having tied a rope round
    the neck of the dog.
We must have been quite out of breath, with all that singing
    and dancing!

I pretended not to know, despite the fact that I knew.
When I realized it was my turn, I started shaking like crazy.

We must have been quite out of breath, with all that singing
and dancing!
The birds were singing, and the flowers were blooming. The sky
was high, and the ocean was deep.

When I realized it was my turn, I started shaking like crazy.
We laughed so hard even our stomachs hurt.

The birds were singing, and the flowers were blooming. The sky
was high, and the ocean was deep.
As you can see, we were now facing a difficult situation.

We laughed so hard even our stomachs hurt.
When I was very pleased to see someone, I cried.

II.

INSIDER

This is what it means to move out of one's
body: to split today into order, uncanny condi-
tions. This is what it means to touch the dead
"what we spoke of" at the heart of ordinary life:
that the mind eats the body, the body does not
eat the mind. As if all along we'd been dressed
in it, taking everything to heart, desire called
up in a shadow of leaves, dark prodigy of all
we knew. New skin, new company received,
half-eaten light in a primrose void. Whoever
was not laughing would become dense, amidst
the laughing. And through this natural mag-
ic one's body, simply moving, would fold into
those forces to which it was drawn. As if peo-
ple were to be blamed for being people, rath-
er than faculties (the fish and the gods); as if
every word forgotten meant there were not a
thousand muscles in the eye. A voice comes
to one, the legs hang down in the dark, and
neither body nor soul forgets anything, in the
manner of a good host. Something happens,

the song returns—and are you asking me what it means? To live freely, inside this house? All I have experienced is so far gone within me: the log becomes the ash or doesn't, the air foams up, the sky calls down and speaks sea. And that's always what it's like, when I like it, still talking, making talk for the tenuous thought that anything whatever stays cold, and loves to breathe. As if to be replaced by that desire, repelling speech, to echo the glossy nothing of that good and inexhaustible dream: how it hurt me, the sound of those words, licked as a cow licks her calf, how I dropped to my knees beside the bed and understood myself as my own, a wet knot of thread. Yesterday I was influenced, a day or two later some premonition sets me down. And here where I am now I write to you, transported, the door to error open, having gradually become the subject of that "natural" I will finally let trace my lips. With this inside music, with this ghost of a smile smiled the way everything unto substance is born: from window to bewildered circle, from kindness into milk cut with rain. Bored in English, bored while running. Or else chewing each separate happiness into its own corpse of light, and fearing nothing but thinking, the thin walls of this augmented house.

Meanwhile we were most often connected by habit. It was the strangeness in me that carried us back out of that milieu. To remember how it was meant meant suffering, meant my reflection's living scrawl became that body lit-up inside, that body you would love and in loving would not possess. And just like that, all those who were wicked left bigger than when they'd arrived. And the tossed-off curve of the mountain enfleshed its sentences with all-but-words. When I wake in the morning and forget who I am, that terror's as real and stark as a dream's: with dark gentleness the spider pits, with circumlocutions their limbs. Once there were two hatreds, the old woman said, then there were worlds upon worlds. It's a pain, but you can always find a place. The muteness of the diary ruins its correspondent. I woke up, thought of moments to invent, a method, a pictured idea. A squirrel fell out of a tree and hissed, big and mangy. And in the softness of the afternoon light even that was urgent with grace. As if struck in the back of the head the story occults its other, self-corrupts back into dream. As if now it were spring, the lion, etc. As if I'd held your hand in the shower, held up your hair in the street. To cook it on high, to see it stays locked when the light turns red. You'll see a dog outside, hear something like breathing, a noise. The way broke on a cold Sunday the wind slips in: like a dancer's body, like something to say. Like in the teeth of a terrible storm that rigid and difficult grace. So warmth becomes suspicion, the spring our early bright doom. In the garden a stretch of life, faint memory, expulsion-as-pain. What in the implausibly open bad of the year the air comes to terms with as rain, the you-of-wind. Or the way outside for all to see (in that era of latex and ink) like a singular, miraculous hand our wiser icons spilled into variants, pretended questions, into the living-hair scent that seems always to presage the return of ideal life. In the semi-flesh of the widening dream, in the long divine of the ceaseless itself. And thus the pulse of the sensory returns, the morning's rose fires peek in through the opening door. As when the morning is cold, a red particular, and I as a mystery wake vastly to myself in darkness, impossible wind.

My voice at once humorous and painful, my delight in consciousness and my fear of it. That summer sun would rise, wreathed in mist, and its affectionate, doggish warmth was a kind of learned helplessness. There was a point to this ritual, which was embarrassment, theme of memory: the numbing of the brain that loves. Wetly I declared my hindsight, in the first blast of wind closed the last of my drawers. It was a day like any other (game of moods), in which I seated myself, penciled in; it was one epoch the growing teeth of which I would have passed without understanding. Having spoken myself through them, having been strange atop the weight of that ground. And through my own eyes having known the clumsiness of a life bearing out, the labored O of a mouth mouthing "born, born, born." At that our great cries went up, cries which even then we knew were only the dead tracing dully their feelings of open love: the looking trap, "criminal peace," sweet terrors held big and aloft. Wherever the water faced flowed compassion, and the crust of that filling surpassed whatever in our weakness would tempt us. Intimate distance, things and words. The darkness that would cover the law after the eleventh, the thirteenth, the eighth. For whom the body was "thou," the red heart was "thee." For whom the danger that colored space was sacred and, like blood flecked with light, understood. And this in itself was a way of knowing everything, a way of being coveted, known and apart. One speaks oneself, and in speaking says, "of, of, another." That I am trembling and confused is not your opening (whatever one thinks, what the moon is like, not liking to know in his changing shape the stranger, not liking to hold that gun). It is good with two halves of a face to fall open, merely fabricated, to say to one's widening body that the future, too, would kill to set up at that crossroads. Which is the end of everything, even if good: the natural breathing between the flesh (knowing everything) and what it was like to wake up in that bed: tossed and reeling, a horror with money, those half-human eyes spanning hundreds of years.

Having thought there was something pleasant in the smell of old trash, "some sweetness, some life." That there is change and then there is change, conditions passing, that long grey warbling on which one breaks one's teeth. One ghost throws out the other, laughing, sees in the mirror the shape of her dream. Per sitting, one contact, per color one incidental twist. Urgency of tables, catastrophe of bricks: this one neat trick by which I like a woozy dog call up a grey sun, chalky and cold as inedible rice. Dislodged I'd think passage, concluded dream the water off my skin. For a time among my friends I was a legend; it was simple enough to recklessly fly off, eager head in the lion's warm mouth. In the stretch of our unbecoming becoming drafty, all cat, in the first of a series of long days wet from end to spoken end: I was into it, am still, wouldn't be here opening windows if not. It is eerie to live, eerie to breathe. It is a kind of eating to stand this close to you, writing fire, imparting heat. And then suddenly in the workings of that operation you see a grace, a natural possession, each point of light settling in like a hand into crushed ice. And it would be just like that (I know it) to walk toward you, loving and convinced, in all the obvious parts of space to arrive like a bedroom, a screen. In the subway lucid, warping space, with that kind of lurid smile by which surprise plays tag with reason, always wins. But I am rarely this good, am alien to what is. Where the lips meet, at the falling away. To lose sleep in the intimacy of glass (that pressing need), to be sluggish and shaking and thus understood. That there is light and then there is light, held in greeting. That like the feeling of frozen hair the substance of the text is only necessary, the world we have. There is what for example the arrow makes real, some poignance, a sharper last breath. This welcome look returned by the screen, a breath that engenders its supplement out of consensus, the trash of surprise. Because I will or I won't, having existed, go to bed anymore, and never sleep. Because it will only get harder to be kind in this language, or sweet, in this silence grown subtle and mean. That is, to be breathing again, though at heart a killed darkness, a *no* in one distant world and in another a thing mouthing life. Which is always what happens, when the hand sinks in. Like a fleet of great mackerel, heavily parabled, in a dark akin to someone, akin to me: from two salty eyes grow the mask, and everything within me hating what I desire, which is time, and only time. That the smell of the sea is already blue, and still speaking, that the winding circle of cold mountains picturing a middle death will in the end be the delight that fills us. Like pictures of storms, teeth slick as eels, as what one prefers of the obvious falls in with a realizing grace. Not in life but in dreams, not in the world but in the line of that world's abstraction: coiled and thinking, alive in that egg.

Yet it wasn't easy, having not had enough. The facts in which you dwelled grew cool and, as promised, severe. Here was that trust you felt, held fast by the weight of those others. And the more deeply that powder was rubbed in the more quickly it became your story, a body that in its uncertainty would radiate outward, forgetting its structure, warming the air. That river was inclusive, and visible, and like the thirsting throat of a reptile spread from moment to moment, to its marrow a real child, a jealous spring. And just as sensation gives into distance, that virtual body was unpronounceable. And the truth that comes from stories—which is old, and shakes for anything—was inside of what just a moment earlier was so prolonged: that I was there, that I was in that night, in the mirrors a form of stillness, in the syllables a soundless wave. I would face this question, but not to ask it; I would allow myself this moniker, and look out from this personable skull. There was a moment when I believed it—on the narrative's edge, warm in the light of my personal brand. And then a trickle of consciousness, like a shower of dark-red curls, awakened to form, and as that figure swam blearily out of its present and into my past I couldn't help but feel, with its hand in my hand, with every burst of rain the dumb return of that slow face. "To be a ghost is to know no pain," to vomit in peace, wherein these words, the cool of their associate woods. And then a line is added, an hour to cling to. And then this I who asks and attends would surrender its death, and live in you, and lie down in the written-on earth.

And how was it then that I felt? Being born with such indefinite features, with secret scenes recited quickly to myself from the insides of facts. And from the egg of that fullness I grew severely, and rounded the earth; I put the dumb spirit to sleep and became the animal that un-zeroes the world, molecular and free. This was the game we thought the night was, the bruise we hadn't yet seen. It was hard in the thematized body to make terms with exhilaration. It was hard to be alone, harder to insist on death—which was the mystery, and the bite bearing down, and a thousand songs soaked through to their roots, and big with light. And whatever still moved would inherit it, this moment of rivers. And whoever thirsted with the throat of the waking earth would gather courage to grow a body, then bathe it in air. There is this music which ends the world, which we called life, and turned toward with love. And it was easy enough to admire the ghostly note of that promised spring. For this was the hearer of that voice that renews our affections, a baby of degree telling time in the afternoon. Of the maternal shambles, naturally, of the way the text feels distant, and loved, like an unraveling shore, and how every feeling with the prelude of second skin discovers in composition the arc of this small kindness: the flash of the maximum, of awkward sapien strength. Such is this process, which kills well to stay alive, and would be simple enough, in the twelfth month, the fifth, the third, to match itself in severity, knowing the freedom that is exhaustion amidst the eruption of emotive demands. And such is the dreamer who finds it (exquisite to never have it), lifting nothing into that long white film whose ocean like an open face the wind burns, with internal pressure, along this plane or that alien segment in deep burning air. And gradually what little there is files into the opening present: reality by reality, a cool web of tongues, that severe and infinite figure for what it is to have lived, and talked a body ashore. You lie down in this, in the general murmur. And then the wind as unheard music glosses time, and the past you know you are is thus believed.

III.

WILD NEWS

Because in the actual beginning.
Because in the midst of the seam.
Where the tree's
Rotting ground the purple had dreamed

Out of then into life,
As window as branch-
Made time is mastered effect—

Because nothing is thread-
Bare waiting because the mercy is not
Already so with what
Oh, detested, part-secret
Pleasure running up & back of it.

With a screech not whole nor shadow of
Waving plenitude,

With that sheet that corresponds itself
With life, the everything said.

How obvious & ugly the capital is
(This capital)
How sacred in it those who lose sleep.

On the verge of refusal petals drooping
Onto faces the gods all want
To see vivid with actual flame,

The subject stance
To recall its own lightning, to see in this
The fable of the dark therein—

Which is a kind of courage
Now & rotting
Which is life itself
Extending murmured trunk to murmured brain.

Until & against the thing it is,
The everything soft from shadows born—
To be & have from terror's

Rustic sweetness
An invented love
To glide along

An obvious mind
Nearly granted a salt-
Water night that lives well
In the crush of escape

From which the moment that kills
Goads writing this sentence this life

Into middle-death
Of sweetness at home of myself
In a warmer skin—

At odds with life and entire
As time which compels one to speak

The quiet touch
Of sought love what the world repeats

Beginning:
That having is only meanness,
That writing is being & not
Not giving, only more

As with the body in its call to kill
In its natural valley that single good
& woozy image

That white aluminum
Ocean's sun

That thought wears, breathing
As the earth does between its parts.
To remember the ends
Lived back to their beginnings,

To remember in the line
Of one eye erasing

How hard it is
In ardor to discern that reluctance to die—

As you remember it there
A habit of flesh

An eagerness
Of slow pain a brightness thought deep
That in particular speaks of its end:

Some empty nothing strangely made

For what was and could
Reopen

Into an I inside
A soft white tongue

Into no life
Not desired nor in either
Direction not filled.

When I think of what consciousness is.
Half-hearted, lit together.

When I think of the world
The world lives in
How it embroiders its sweetness with fear.

That anyone-scream, the spoken thing
Which is enormous & outside courage:

To find what it is, what promise
In the belly of human joy, what restless
& happy person there is

Who by descending makes everything sharp
& sweetly real

Who like a probable life
Leans in toward forgiveness

In an impossible
Sweltering sky the night's
Calm dream called back
From that country called I-of-air.

To explain what it is
That I who am only nothing would be
Read slowly when gradually opened

A parody of reactive
Mantra loving otherwise loving years

As kindness with soft
Insistence effects that story
The breath is born to:

A something-canticle, closed-mouth amen,
An astonishment
That languages sleep a green &
Opening happiness

That as the spirit moves
Literal over the dark's soft face
Where one secret embraces its counterpart

In the great human un-
Adulterated of life past life

Makes a harmony of face
To near-face makes an idea of what I am

As just that being, as thought
Ending there with *river*
River now.

When I am in it
Up to the lips with thirst
To be over and again that thing
Wordless and recomposed

That large and conscious breathing
Which is everyone in this room,

Which is the birds themselves
Hottest with summer's continuance

Never knowing the other only seeing
A string of faces skeptical & wise

In desire's tiny sun a thought of trees
& muddy water,
A me in another creatured life
Calm & astonished to feel it:

An entire day
Remote with continuous beauty, a wanted
Transmutation

Which is waking, & finding light
In the life the heart would lead

Where only absence is
Impossible, a laugh
Like oats with salt

Where what it is to live
Is in living to not yet know
What escapes the story's telling
From plexus to naked arm

& where to move
Toward you is to wander
That desert in which these fruits are preserved

Into that spoken thing
Only now created
That opens out into every room.

& the dream arrives alone
Remaining movement

    & utterly the mind
    In its time of reading discerns this need—

To be a sculpted haunt
Among spasms, bursts,

A plate & a little spoon
Becoming tyrants in their arena.

& then in a light like the flapping of wings
Downhill with glinting leaves & coat pulled tight
You summon yourself as such
Into the line the body became

    As the morning wills the air to move
    & slowly burn

    & the face that always pleases
    Tells the story of what one needs:

That there is a world in this
Like birds in sentient wind

That there is today & the urge
To miss it

      As a miracle in the height of summer twists
      Into appetite knowing sleep.

      That there is a body inside experience
      With a bowl for a mouth
      & a sound for an inflorescence,

Where the pieces render
In high vibrato
& all the names you don't

Insist on grow up & die
Remain with you
As definite goods—

Sprung from theft & inner life
Or else by force of habit set ablaze.

& from time to time
With one foot planted in that sort of life
A part of me turns
As if from within, needling

Thought into the earlier quiet telling
Of those trees on the stroke of horizon
Flecked with spittle & wet grey light.

& these little words
Are made to feel unnatural
& that their ooze in the fullness of air's
All pupil & prior

The clouds toward which we wing
& double back.

All shattering involves
Life & all life the sinking of love
Into shadowy distinctness.

& I confess it with all my force
Under this prospect, with no moon to speak
These mountains & common rivers

& think of the world we become when we become
Immaterial as what we love

As the roadside the skylarks
The stones like tiny white knives

Across each listening moment
Of accent & nothing created.

Because the time never arrives
In November, because the wind shakes
Everything beyond now & then

& I remember myself
As the food of that place
"Listen" I want to laugh "Listen"

Even weakly, that the forehead kissed
Follows first, that the edge is
Exhorted to bliss & is peculiar

In that it functions
"Sensitive to the entire body"
& made of flowers to evoke a flood.

But I do not want to be
Inside this obvious machine

Of foreheads contingent & vast
Brought drunk to the mistake that is
This story its purple deep

As an almost-human
Kindness the dream pulls
Out of the mouth.

& the flames curl
Wetly the wings of these kairoi the national dream
Is words is a certain fatigue.

& then the wind is quiet
& I can think again
With flesh & soft light of brain

"Which always remembers
the wind that shook it"
The hands and feet

Of branches, their names
Recalling order
In ordinary light.

& thus to listen
To every you
In front of someone

Among the stumps the fat waves
Of clover

Learning more & more
To shoulder that ugly
Wealth & its sensation of itself

As an oil of current that flows
Into its ecstasy & will not die.

& therein the body has its face,
& therein the story proclaims its telling

Of no void
Not set in motion, of no sweetness in the tendons of this
Bright lattice

This geometry of light
In structured air.

& I would crawl into bed
Forever to grow as ripe as that

I the music I the air not yet
Not dead, with a headache & no
Body yet to tell it to

How to erupt & draw the milk I mean
From everything

When the nerves are slow
& this house is not a house

But Greek & variable, a brain of sun
& tongue & paint & light.

I was there then
& I saw it in some way

Or I was next
To it, as one of many
Open eyes with-

Held in open air.
& I could have starved to death

Thinking I needed that
As a ray of light & living nerves
Is a fire the brain moves through

Caressing the walls
To marry that terror
To certainty, to error a weakening sun.

It makes me nervous
To be inside this story

With you under this copper
Sky from which a big blonde
Ink pours reliably over the earth.

& we would move in this
As incarnate persons
As immanence machines

Dropping blossoms for human trees
In this long moment of nausea
In this harder moment of grace

Wherein if the dead no longer
Vomit they do still love
To connect the edges

Inside experience
Like little gods
Who turn from us to speak

From where in the future the past
Takes place not
Yet devoured, a cold blue
Intimacy of throat & soft
Speech. & I'll have recalled this

Awake all night & flagrant
Becoming as snow that melts
In the afternoon sun

& as in each puddle a spray of eyes
Blinks back to me the prettiest
Cawing gale, so the flesh

Of the hands in the moan of the storm
Is true, & set in motion

Like some complete & loved
Rotation of talk
& hard sun

& would imprint upon
The visitant earth
That heat & that compounding

Sweet note
Of florid rot

Through which this light would run
Which is the living meat
Of April & the ghosts thereof.

& I will remember
What I can remember
Waking in the room the thought
Of such & such,

That a hot cloud covered the sky wherever
In time before was flat.

& elsewhere having known it
Dying twice in the charming air
That in this soft hand the lines are good
That in this little

Basement the tasteless fruit of time
In horror pulls back
The shades of a dinosaur's dream.

& then the thing says
Attractively I am with you
Inside this idea
Which is a feeling

Do you remember
That below that
Is another feeling
Wet hair on the winter deck

As now & again as now, for this
Indulgence howling into shape

Is a paper house that blossoms
& is real, & will extract from you
No light.

& now I myself am weak
& thus essential

As weightless
As capital is death

Breathing white
Performance watching life

Between invisible hands
In orbit & not unmoved.

This is the variant
In our emptiness
The morning's blank
Everything on the edge of a tongueless wind.

Because the road is dreaming
& disappointed

Because the sun just
Shaken awake has a body
Of silhouette all its own

I will incline myself to learn
Though spoiled, I will collect
Myself & inch

Outside finding
In oddness sweet
Attunement

To that fraction of attention along what curve
Hid from light that births the chaos of spring.

Where among the good the air is dry
When we are dead the willing mud—

    In the pollen of common
    Flowers, smoke
    Of a quiet afternoon.

To watch it
With perfect comprehension, the weakness
Of a thing forming love.

Out of world
& blind skin
With the wind in the heart's upending—

With living snow
In fragmented wild
Light crowding the least decayed

Almost-corpse the soil makes.

To wake in pain & light,
A non-production
Of images silence breaks

Into that star within
Presence that asks
Is it really myself
In this scene turned pale

In this permission from which fountains rise—

Having swallowed at each
Horizon whence mystery whence pleasure

As that strangeness obedient to what "I"
I believed with infinite mistaken
Intensity to be the intimate sound

Of hooves somnambulant & wise

Becomes the question itself
Expanding
Into pure yes without reason.

& then what one is with pleasure is brought raw to
the altar.
& the sun pulls down the wide lips of the day

As evening drops
Into understanding born
Alive, a silent & pink absolute:

That this even now is coherent, that what holds
Confusion from grasp to next breath
Is from room to deep room moving

Full of fear
& loved invention

More eerie maternal epic
Half-pulverized & in that inner

Deep like memory

Along the contours of that person
To move the way the eye makes pictures

As the meadow's
Long body already
With strangeness moves from joy
To fused description

The sparkling waves crashing & raw

    As the sky falls away to my right
    & the moving air like a low fire waves
    Much compelled with the pulse of coming dusk.

    & from the cold floor then knowing
    What's ahead
    I like a sounded flower hear repeating

What I had wanted others to know
A roar of applause
That ends in alarm   for no life

In yonder woods no wafting
Of that element into
The ghostly psychological my opposite
Harbored in mud—

    As the shining body sways
    Between nothing & what it is called
    Knowing what a frightening thing it is

To walk   becoming verdigris
A living place
In which one ghost to another confides

How impossible it is to refuse
With agony what the air turns in   How after fusing
Together the bones of the thing

The house will accept the wind
Into this creatured dream in which we'll find each other

Well-drawn & alive, real copies
Of those things we remember

Opening slowly in personal light.

Into something I ask to be melted.
Into two languages
Inside my head split with gold
In the clearness of air.

& this lump of red
Flesh is distinctly kindred.
& my toes are in the water
Where the long turn is

Afraid of distance so pretty
With hesitation.

A pair of nice hands
In all things is what
We think tonight

From the inside
Out where the soil in its power admires

The thought of the bud
That remembers & then is nervous
To flay the wind.

& figment
Going further is motion,
& the blue house

With good reason diverges from
My company, & space
As if having kindled many fires

In semi-invented
Shadow makes no new
World to so prolong.

I would ask to be melted.
I would so state facts
As to make me that story

Where out of some picture a line is born
As a voice on a bus at night
Or a train

In sepia parade
& let this knot of dread

& quiet promise fall over every
Inch of what the flesh would know

In this weather of continuous
Coolness & passing lights

Where what occurs to me
Is a light that breathes
& speaks to pass the night

A bland & true
Dream of where the words will go

Of what & who my nothing
Shall greet me with, believing it still

Impossible & serene
My image
The thing that pleases

My own paltry
Opposite with throat & dark survey.

Then in or reversed, maybe back, I'll float,
So obviously having given
Myself the marked feeling of "dead"

Various fire, having called "I"
The dim ghost of the body,

All soils
The poem envelops *sweet break*
In the unlocked skin.

& then I am calm, & in the room
Whatever else loves nervously admires
What the neck sees, what the true spine

Which would be friend to the world
Constructs in this space
In the manner natural to human speech.

It is good when this happens.
It is good to find nothing
Where everything was

As the breath continues
& the little voice that is
The body's on the floor of this
Bright fiction will slip
Out of the brain, then in again

Feeling despite itself its old habits
Devolve into motley, simple Gomorrah
Of good taste as all ugliness is

Productively expressed   in spring
& attends to me
With such cool & viscous regard.

The flower parts
At the base, the human face
Is truer than that real one there

Which is obscure
& snakes along

Like rows of mirrored
Wheat the contours of
The scream of the rising moon
For our reference, & edification

& as bad as it is
Still dreaming I grant this structure
The breath it needs.

To bear this noise
& so to take the measure of that
Motion that would observe us

On the rim of the egg, upended,
Having died, in the long serene
Everything that turns in early

Though it barely has time to breathe:
That concept betrays
By its arrival, & the dry core

Of what we really wanted,
Crushed & supersonic,

Is the silence the world is like—
Or is a crane with its egg, its ache
Ultravisible & happy

& which with soft
Exactment births a world well in touch with our needs.

About what little I remembered, even that
I feared: the future's sea-thick reach
A refuge, sometimes slow, sometimes near.

The way a perfect feeling lands
& then discovers us, indulges along
Each precipice our precise & illegible blanks—

Just so in trouble like myself a smile drifts
With the sun behind it
With the faint blush or yellow red
Of some planted independence quiet flesh.

The way a child speaks
When bored but still
In comfort a long way off

I turned my reflection
& my brain into dusky light
Into the air that glows
In the periphery where the sentence seeks

My first heat of shadow, my being
Worked open supervisible night & day—

As if from the very first
Landing I was impossible, a landed "no"
Cooked slow into butter a record of will

With walls like
Shoulders along the snowy edge
Of raised feelings

      With which plus just a throat you raise a house
      Happy & free as distance
      & a breathing

& regulated vastness becomes a sky deep and speaking
The bid of its own white sea—

      To story the violent earth
      To abandon

Comprehension to whatever for itself
Into the eye of death recounts

That this is what it is
To make silence
Speak, what excites
Along the lip of clenched

Possibility serenely all evening a life
That sweetly rises

 As a terror of wind
 A body of leaves
 A shock

Of skin that loves the sun, what in the beginning forgave me
 my name

Re-fleshed & obedient, an open
Weight with which to break one's heart—

 As every stop aggrieves
 That "me" upstairs in blood pursuit

Of what it's like to be dying
And not even tired

Of whatever it is
Inexorable with "God" some violent game
Of semblance unthinking the world—

 With this stride that paces my morning
 With this insistent excitement in flames

Bright-naked & solar, strong & with
Dread to bend toward it

With the question of whether I live
Taking aim.

I was trying, & I got so close
& it was carried away with me
To get to sleep.

I saw the flowers grow
Tiny on the horizon & much
Of open autumn

Until the crows stopped
Cawing & remembered the wind
That knew them.

& even that was personal.
& I would have crawled all aft-
ernoon to pass once more through this

With you, I who was barely
Chronological in my season.

Because it was good to have courage
& body body, & ugly the water.

Because Hell was the Garden &
Repeatedly so

On the kitchen floor
In the lifting up of sleep-
Laden glass.

& so moved I would in time
Have been native to that little dream

In which I like a slow
Wave made everything happen.

Which is the play of this art
Completely
In the dark to the sweet
Compounding of one's demons

On whom nothing is lost
With gold in the sky
& clear in the blood-winged air.

I was trying, I was carried
I was making a soft

Figure for the hand that would
On the surface, for a time, would almost
Each time mark the dim still-
Speaking of

The weather the birds what valley
I woke up nervous in.

& I didn't even have one,
A nature, dead not dead

& I in life
Would state facts & pour them out
No flowers
& still in air—

I was the study of this
With the hand & the kind
Delta of that cheek
On my cheek

I was the body in the meat of its own
Constellation, where I found you
Having become that thing

Where I was
& while I waited

Inside of that
Wherein in each sweet
Note the fear of blood

& tongue & clarity, that fear of simple
Nothing & yet too old to fear.

I was not yet asleep, yet I slept
Playing every note
Myself & still denying it.

That we are our own
Though we have not yet
Made up our minds

To break into pieces
& thus to peer out from behind
The book to watch the roaches die
In ecstasy hot on the rotting sill.

In this house we recognize order
& are Greek for this, or birds.
The soul of the animal is beautiful.

Three years ago, ten years ago, I'd go
With you prolonged as the shadows of
What I was to it
From an upturned blossom.

& it would not be easy
To call to you
When the lights come on

To doze & wake
& call it Hölderlin
(*For there we found but you*)

Call it memory, milk & paradox—
Where the trance of the instant
Grows brightest

& would mortgage its life
To stay strange.

What some call
God is simply an imitation
Of these requirements.

O weakness, to never slow down
Though faced with the bloody gel
Of days   In that slow
Rotation what you give to me

Drains the very fluid from
My eye.

What other hell
Would see this through?
Dark like a strange
Interment, lovely & deep

A pearling gum
Of light through dripping trees.
& whatever I did I did
Without knowing why.

For the work has no end,
It is ugly here

Yet the source of all magic
Over the mountains
Through the pines
Accordingly, no moon.

& it is both physically & morally true
That in your presence no part

Makes all,
That it is yours as much as it is
Theirs that it has

As little relation to words
As the stones we heat in the fire

To convey affection to our friend
The night.   No other hell
Departs from me.

Yet now I feel like dancing.
This pain is not
Memorable enough to be
Auspicious.

I note that the birds here don't fly off
At first sight of new snow.
I count the birds,

The beautiful birds
Who agree with me.
There's no such thing as prose.

Then the sun & the wind
& the rain came here
& were alive with a great

Emptiness. Like half-open
Mouths the flowers wept.
& I waited & waited

Until the scenery changed
& the first birds
That thus came to me were a bewilderment

Of vision
& tore into the walls of my heart.

All over the body
Is hard to remember.
& what I call myself thus

Disintegrated is
The shaking of
The pleasure of being
Seen luminous, as through an egg.

O whatever that is, I have seen it
It lives, forms pointlessly
In clouds around

A given object
A living branch whose telos is
To speak, a little laughter
To which we can't help but surrender our love.

& yet still murky
Of only words
The fact grows
Instanter

In its strangeness
& the forgeries that do not
Hurt you sleep apart from the remembered world.

That music hums
Enormous from deep inside
The lake.

It must be warm to feel so
Particular. The brave
Mute smile that shouts
Its little formation

Says that I am, am yours
Imperatively so
Here where the sun is of no
Location

& the wind that harries
Our outlines is
Like anything we do
In the meat of the heart

Startled in freedom, the grace
Of entrails snapping into place

Saying dreams are the only things
That interest us
As we smile to ourselves

& bend with the curve
Of time
The way the bird commonly called

The robin pries wide its beak
For minutes beyond force, & trembling.

NEGATIVE LIGHT

Now that I am home,
I persevere, in my dream
in which I am like a fresh-cut
sprig saying hello to you.

And the question lingers, and the house is my refrain,
unfolding mystery
out of persona: yellow moon
in the river, meat packed
in living snow.

It falls to us, the sky,
coming down for us
with something wicked.

And the woods provoke us, and the language
of appearance is sleepless, beloved,
suddenly magical with dark intent,

like a mist that makes in slow feedings
sweet the soft skin, sweet the sharp
and woody air.

And shall we not go back there,
from our commotion,
by moonlight to pluck from it
something new?

So many things grow estranged.
The second person, for example,
who is elsewhere and does not belong
to "me." As incompletely the hair,

incompletely the teeth.
As when from a distance we recognize
that all-strangeness, constantly stranger,
which is the friend to which we return:

the driven quarry, the lushly evil woods.
My teeth broken and scattered
to figure grace, following the outline of whatever burns.

Let all operations
of the earth be indistinguishable from this,
as the darkness of the original rides its cloud
dayward, and the skull renews its softness in warm milk.
And in the dark like a newborn

half-shade may I collect this truer crop,
with cardamom pods, with myrrh.

Such an encounter leaves behind its earthy residuum.
These and other images arrive,
having passed into this blank
geography, as if they would summon a city there.

And there the years move
darkly into force, and the idea
of the sky by claim of flaw

or failure
sinks into the scruffs of our necks
and carries us off.
May all that it is
to be alive be held there,

in that image device.
And may the future
such as it is, squirm open.
And may we arrive there without ourselves.

NOTES

The English counterparts of the Korean poems "놀이터," "본 국," and "극락" are "Playground," "Native Country," and "Pure Land," respectively. The English and Korean versions of these poems correspond closely and can be thought of as translations, although they were composed simultaneously. Most of the text is adapted from example sentences found in *Korean Grammar for International Learners* (Ihm, Hong, & Chang, 2009), the *Daum* online Korean-English dictionary, and other sources.

The phrase "the scenery, when it is truly seen, reacts on the life of the seer" comes from the journals of Henry David Thoreau.

The phrase "Sensitive to the entire body" comes from the *Ānāpānasati Sutta.*

The phrase "somehow oozed on" is adapted from a sentence in Beckett, *Worstward Ho.*

The lines "In the end what stands out is the green mountain, / the cloud drifting across it" are adapted from a poem by Lady Ōtomo no Sakanoe (trans. Rexroth):

> *Do not smile to yourself*
> *Like a green mountain*
> *With a cloud drifting across it.*
> *People will know we are in love.*

ACKNOWLEDGMENTS

Thank you to the editors of *On the Seawall*, the *Small House Pamphlet Series*, *Sink Review*, *Visible Binary*, and *Action, Spectacle*, where earlier versions of some of these poems first appeared.

Thank you to my friends, with special thanks to John Cotter, Graham Foust, Elisa Gabbert, Jae Kim, Sueyeun Juliette Lee, Erinrose Mager, Jeffrey Pethybridge, Joshua Ware, and CL Young for providing help, encouragement, and audience.

Thank you to Shane McCrae for believing in the book, and to Caryl Pagel and Hilary Plum for shepherding it into existence.

Thank you, always, to my parents.

Michael Joseph Walsh is a Korean American poet
and the editor of *APARTMENT Poetry*.
He lives in Denver.

RECENT CLEVELAND STATE UNIVERSITY POETRY CENTER PUBLICATIONS

Edited by Caryl Pagel & Hilary Plum

POETRY

for a complete list of titles visit csupoetrycenter.com